1 *There are many ways of completing this question. The specimen completion below would receive full marks.* (15)

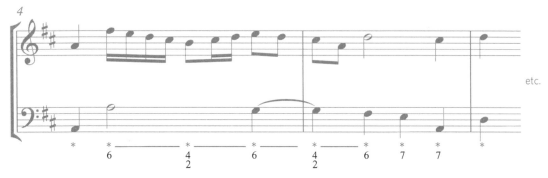

2 *There are many ways of completing this question. The specimen completion below would receive full marks.* (15)

3 *There are many ways of completing this question. Either of the specimen completions below would receive full marks.* (20)

EITHER

(a) *Source (adapted): Schumann, Romance from Album for the Young, Op. 68*

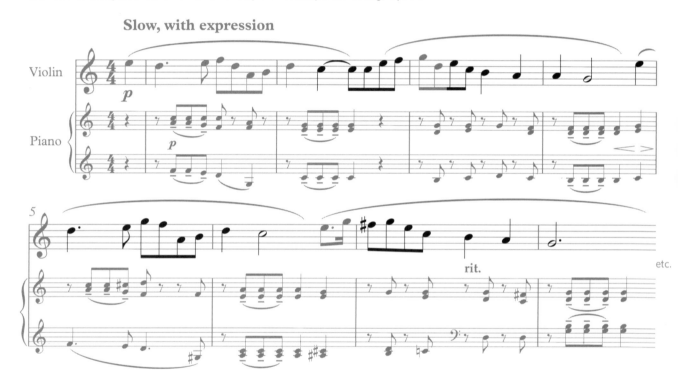

OR

(b) *The given opening is printed in grey in order to distinguish it from the completion, but candidates must include the given opening in their answer.*

oboe

4 *Source: Haydn, 'She never told her love', Hob. XXVI/34*

(a) very slowly / extremely slowly / slow enough / sufficiently slowly / very stately / extremely stately (2)

(b)  (3)

(c) Bar 9   diminished 7th / vii°⁷c / VII⁷c diminished (3)

    Bar 15   V⁷a / V⁷a major (3)

(d) *All possible answers are shown on the extract reproduced below and on page 6.*

  B Bar 7 (2)

  C Bar 6 (2)

  D Bar 19 (2)

  E Bars 20–21 (2)

  F Bars 12–15 (2)

  G Bar 15 (2)

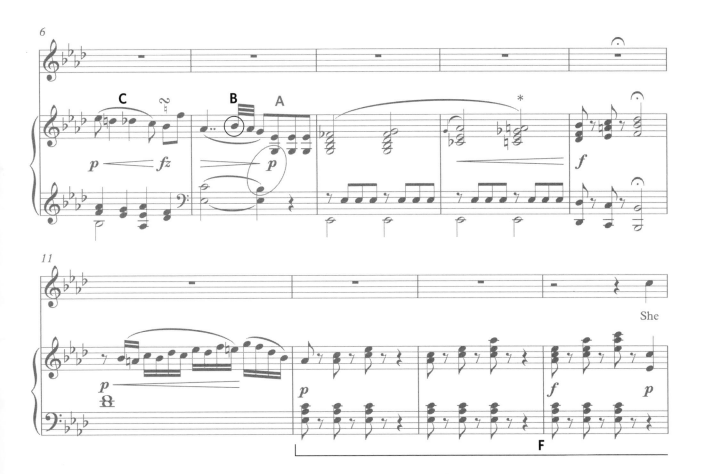

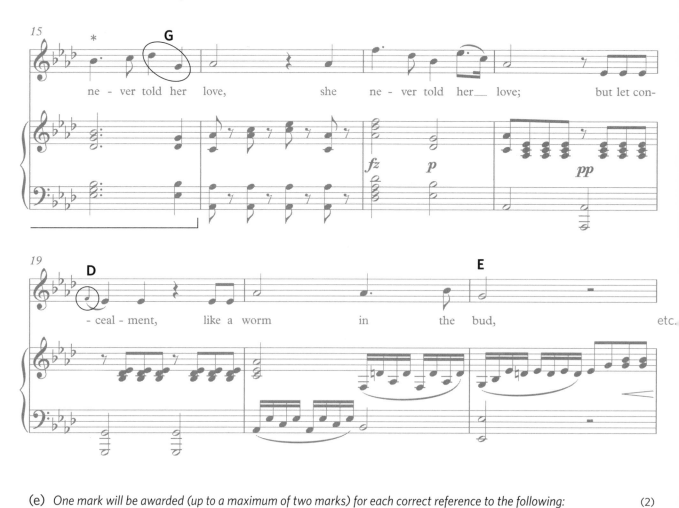

(e) *One mark will be awarded (up to a maximum of two marks) for each correct reference to the following:* (2)

harmonic language / use of dynamics / classical accompaniment style / pianistic style

5 (a) at a very moderate speed (2)

mutes (2)

divided / divided into two parts (2)

(b) (i) (4)

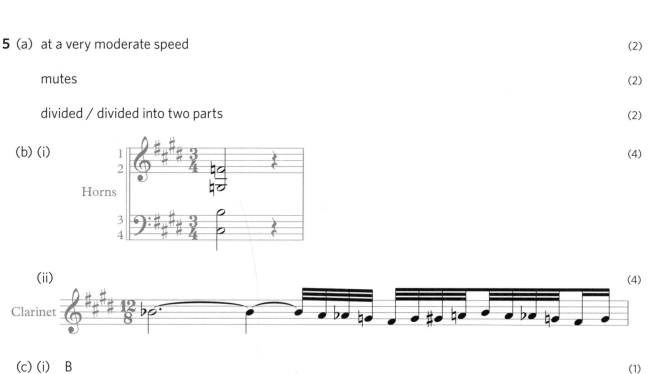

(ii) (4)

(c) (i) B (1)

(ii) 3 (2)

(iii) 1 / 4 (2)

(d) true   (2)

(e) 1 diminished 11th / compound diminished 4th   (2)

   2 augmented 4th   (2)

Theory Paper   Grade 7   2017   B
Model Answers

1 *There are many ways of completing this question. The specimen completion below would receive full marks.*   (15)

2 *There are many ways of completing this question. The specimen completion below would receive full marks.*   (15)

3 *There are many ways of completing this question. Either of the specimen completions below would receive full marks.* (20)

EITHER

(a) *Source: Fanny Mendelssohn, 'Italien', No. 3 from 12 Gesänge, Op. 8*

OR

(b) *The given opening is printed in grey in order to distinguish it from the completion, but candidates must include the opening in their answer.*

violin

4 *Source: Ireland, A Grecian Lad, No. 1 from Three Pastels*

(a) Bar 4   V⁷c / V⁷c major

$\quad$(3)

$\quad$Bar 21   diminished 7th

$\quad$(3)

(b) Similarity   rhythm of melody / crotchet rests in bars 1 and 5 / melody in bars 1 and 5 /
$\qquad\qquad$ use of triplets / right-hand articulation

$\quad$(1)

$\quad$*One mark will be awarded (up to a maximum of two marks) for each correct reference to the following:*

$\quad$Differences   dynamics / lower pitch in bar 5 / harmony / rhythm in lower part of bars 2 and 6

$\quad$(2)

(c) *All possible answers are shown on the extract reproduced below and on page 10. For full marks, candidates need to identify only one example of each answer.*

$\quad$**B** Bar 6

$\quad$(2)

$\quad$**C** Bar(s) 6 / 15–16

$\quad$(2)

$\quad$**D** Bars 13–16

$\quad$(2)

$\quad$**E** Bar 11

$\quad$(2)

$\quad$**F** Bar 22

$\quad$(2)

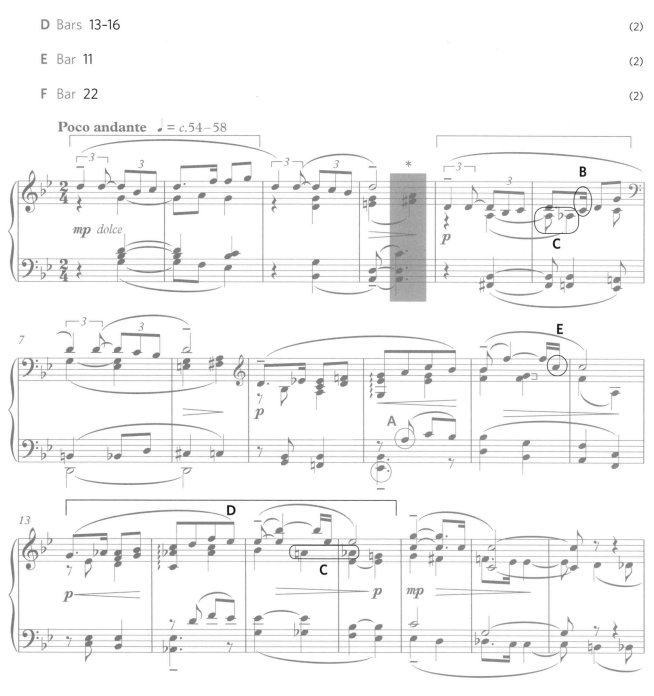

9

(d) 6; 19 (2)

(e) (i) false (2)

    (ii) true (2)

5 (a) or / alternatively (2)

keep with the soloist / with the soloist (2)

repeated semiquavers / measured semiquavers (2)

(b) *One mark will be awarded (up to a maximum of two marks) for each correct reference to the following:* (2)

louder dynamic / higher pitch / delicate orchestration / passionato / double stops in solo violin

(c) (i) (3)

    (ii) (2)

(d) *All possible answers are shown on the extract reproduced opposite.*

B Bar 4 (2)

C Bar 6 (2)

10

(e) **1** major 10th / compound major 3rd   (2)

    2 augmented 9th / compound augmented 2nd   (2)

(f) (i)   true   (2)

    (ii) true   (2)

Theory Paper   Grade 7   2017   C
Model Answers

1 *There are many ways of completing this question. The specimen completion below would receive full marks.* (15)

2 *There are many ways of completing this question. The specimen completion below would receive full marks.* (15)

3 *There are many ways of completing this question. Either of the specimen completions below would receive full marks.* (20)

EITHER

(a) *Source (adapted): Sullivan, 'Fair moon, to thee I sing' from HMS Pinafore*

OR

(b) *The given opening is printed in grey in order to distinguish it from the completion, but candidates must include the opening in their answer.*

flute

4 *Source: J.S. Bach, English Suite No. 4 in F major, BWV 809*

(a) (i) D minor; F major; B♭ major; C major (4)

(ii) 1–4 (2)

(b) Bar 23 iv⁷b / IV⁷b minor / VI⁶a / VI⁶a major

Bar 30 Neapolitan 6th / ♭IIb / ♭IIb major (6)

13

(c)

(d) *All possible answers are shown on the extract reproduced below.*

    B Bar 28   (2)

    C Bar 31   (2)

    D Bars 19–20   (2)

(e) *One mark will be awarded (up to a maximum of two marks) for each correct reference to the following:*   (2)

    use of keyboard / no dynamic markings / harmonic language / contrapuntal texture / use of ornaments / limited keyboard range

5 *Source: Delius, Summer Evening*

    (a) divided / divided into two parts   (2)

    roll / drum roll / rapid reiteration of the same note   (2)

    plucked   (2)

    (b) (i)   (2)

(2)

(c) (i) cellos; violas; third horn (3)

   (ii) 4 / 4-5 (2)

   (iii) 3 / 5 (2)

(d) **1** perfect 4th (2)

   2 major 2nd (2)

(e) (i) true (2)

   (ii) true (2)

Theory Paper Grade 7 2017 S
Model Answers

1 *There are many ways of completing this question. The specimen completion below would receive full marks.* (15)

2 *There are many ways of completing this question. The specimen completion below would receive full marks.*

3 *There are many ways of completing this question. Either of the specimen completions below would receive full marks.* (20)

EITHER

(a) *Source: Schubert, 'Lied der Mignon' from Four Gesänge aus 'Wilhelm Meister', D. 877 (Op. 62)*

OR

(b) *The given opening is printed in grey in order to distinguish it from the completion, but candidates must include the opening in their answer.*

cello

4 (a) Bar 3   V⁷b / V⁷b major   (3)

   Bar 14   diminished 7th   (3)

(b)   (3)

(c) *All possible answers are shown on the extract reproduced below and on page 18. For full marks, candidates need to identify only one example of each answer:*

   B Bar 8 / 10 / 11   (2)

   C Bar 8   (2)

   D Bar 11   (2)

   E Bar 9 / 10   (2)

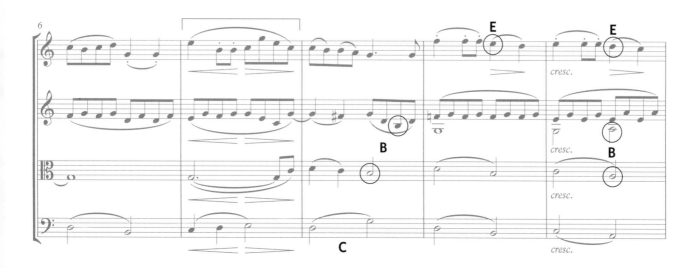

(d) One mark will be awarded (up to a maximum of two marks) for each correct reference to the following:

Similarities   first violin melody / hairpins / harmony   (2)

One mark will be awarded (up to a maximum of two marks) for each correct reference to the following:

Differences   last quaver in viola part / two semiquavers at end of cello part in bar 15 /
phrasing in first violin part / tie in viola part within bar 7 / last two quavers in
second violin part   (2)

(e) (i)   true   (2)

   (ii)   false   (2)

5 (a)   well accented / well marked / well stressed / very emphatic / very accented / very marked /
very stressed   (2)

   on the A string   (2)

   roll / drum roll / rapid reiteration of the same note   (2)

(b)

(3)

(3)

(c) All possible answers are shown on the extract reproduced on the opposite page. For full marks, candidates need to identify only one example of each answer:

   B Bar 1   (2)

   C Bar 1 / 2   (2)

(d) (i)   cellos; trumpet; first horn; second oboe   (4)

   (ii)   1   (1)

(e) **1** minor 13th / compound minor 6th   (2)

   2 minor 7th   (2)

**Supporting the teaching and learning of music
in partnership with the Royal Schools of Music**

Royal Academy of Music | Royal College of Music
Royal Northern College of Music | Royal Conservatoire of Scotland

www.abrsm.org   **f** facebook.com/abrsm
y @abrsm   **▶** ABRSM YouTube

ISBN 978-1-78601-015-5